This paper is part of the
Proceedings
of the
First North-American Conference on Semitic Linguistics
Santa Barbara, California
March 24-25, 1973

T0153725

ON THE ROLE OF PERCEPTUAL CLUES IN HEBREW RELATIVIZATION

Talmy Givón

Department of Linguistics
University of California, Los Angeles

Relativization in Modern Israeli Hebrew is discussed from a number of perspectives. First, it is shown that when the resumptive (anaphoric) pronoun in Hebrew relativization is attracted to the position adjacent to the head noun, the relative subordinator *she-* may be deleted. In other words, the pronoun may assume the perceptual function of relative subordinator. Next, it is shown that the resumptive pronoun itself functions as a perceptual simplifier in relativization, so that when the order of constituents in the relative clause is one which may create ambiguity or difficulty in assigning grammatical relations, the presence of an otherwise optional resumptive pronoun becomes obligatory. This is shown for both subject and object relativization. Further, it is shown that the option of deleting the resumptive pronoun in Hebrew relativization decreases when one goes down the scale of arguments: subject > accusative > simple prepositional objects > complex prepositional objects. This hierarchy is discussed in the context of syntactic-perceptual complexity. Finally, a number of new developments in the marking of relative clauses/pronouns is discussed, particularly the ascendence of the use of WH-pronouns as relative subordinators, and the suppletive effect this process has on the use of the subordinator *she-* and the resumptive pronouns.

TABLE OF CONTENTS

1. PRELIMINARIES

This paper[1] carries on an investigation first begun in Givón (1973). In that paper I have discussed a number of syntactic constraints on relativization in Israeli Hebrew. These constraints involve the relation between two central concepts: SYNTACTIC FREEDOM within the relative clause, and SYNTACTIC/PERCEPTUAL COMPLEXITY of the environment within which the relative clause is embedded. This pertained, first, to the syntactic device known as RE-SUMPTIVE PRONOUNS. It was shown that in more complex environments (with complexity defined, at least initially, in terms of Ross's (1967) COMPLEX NP CONSTRAINT) resumptive pronouns which are otherwise optional in relativization become obligatory. It was also shown that the WORD ORDER FREEDOM of many constituents, including resumptive pronouns, decreases as the complexity of the environment increases. This often results in definite loss of EXPRESSIVE POWER, mostly with respect to topic-comment assignment. It was then argued, along lines similar to those pursued by Keenan (1972), that syntactic devices such as resumptive pronouns as well as the strict adherence to the "neutral" word order, serve to tone down or counter-act the perceptual complexity of the utterance.

In the present paper the interaction between two types of syntactic-perceptual signals used in relativization will be discussed. One is the relative subordinator *she-*, the other is again the resumptive pronoun. It will be shown that a certain trade-off in the deletability of these signals exists, and that within this trade-off the PRINCIPLE OF ATTRACTION, by which relative pronouns or subordinators are positioned directly adjacent to the head noun modified by the clause, plays a governing role. In Givón (1972) I have argued that the attraction principle is motivated by a perceptual need to separate the head noun from the other nominals within the relative clause, in order to maintain the recoverability of the grammatical functions and relations within the embedded clause. This perceptual task is complicated by the ordinary processes involved in forming a relative clause, i.e. deletion, pronominalization and changes in the neutral word order. The data brought out in this paper further support this argument. This paper also suggests, further, that the different prepositional cases in Hebrew have different syntactic/perceptual complexity, and that this complexity affects the syntactic freedom of their corresponding resumptive pronouns in relativization. This may constitute an added, independent support to the findings reported in Givón (1973). Finally, a number of more recent developments within the cluing system of Hebrew relativization will be described and some of their more general implications briefly surveyed.

2. SUBJECT-NP RELATIVIZATION

In languages which posses a "true" relative pronoun, the attraction principle mentioned above applied to that pronoun, in the absence of any other signaling device. However, in languages which posses a relative subordinator distinct from pronouns, the attraction principle applies primarily to that subordinator. Hebrew is a language of the second type, where the subordinator

---

[1]This paper is concerned with spoken Israeli Hebrew and thus requires a brief note concerning dialecticity. The normal native speaker of Hebrew is multi-dialectal in the extreme. He is initially conversant in the more progressive children dialect, roughly corresponding to the "street language" dialect level. Through education, reading and the media he soon becomes conversant with several levels of more literary dialects, some of which are considered appropriate only for writing, radio announcing or--more narrowly--poetry. The syntax, idiom and lexicon of those literary dialect levels harken back, most often, to Biblical, Mishnaic or Talmudic Hebrew. All this makes judgments about "grammaticality," especially in the area of word order options, an extremely involved issue for the native speaker. In this paper I have attempted to make acceptability judgments only in reference to the street-level dialect. In many instances this may mean that a starred sentence is not necessarily "unacceptable" but only "less acceptable" as compared with its unstarred, minimally-paired counterpart.

she- has a fixed position following the head noun and preceding the rest of the relative clause. In the relativization of subject NP's, resumptive pronouns normally do not appear. Thus, for example:

(1) *ha-ish SHE-ba hena etmol baerev*   'The man who came here yesterday evening'
      'the-man THAT-came here yest. eve.'

(2) **ha-ish SHE-HU ba hena etmol baerev*
      'the-man THAT-HE came here yest. eve.'

However, if the neutral S-V-O word order is tampered with,[2] the situation seems to reverse itself and the resumptive pronoun becomes obligatory, as in the case of fronting the direct object, below:

(3) *ha-ish SHE-harag et ha-kelev etmol*   (S-V-O)
      'the-man THAT-killed acc. the-dog yesterday'

      'The man who killed the dog yesterday'

(4) **ha-ish SHE-HU harag et ha-kelev etmol*
      the-man THAT-HE killed acc. the-dog yesterday'

(5) **ha-ish SHE-et ha-kelev harag etmol*   (fronted object NP)
      'the-man THAT-acc. the-dog killed yesterday'

(6) *ha-ish SHE-et ha-kelev HU harag etmol*
      'the-man THAT-acc. the-dog HE killed yesterday'

      'The man who killed the dog yesterday'

The pre-posing of the time-adverb within the clause has a similar though weaker effect:

(7) *? ha-ish SHE-etmol ba hena*
      'the-man THAT-yesterday came here'

(8) *ha-ish SHE-etmol HU ba hena*
      'the-man THAT-yesterday HE came here'

      'The man who came here yesterday'

Thus while (8) above is definitely prefered over (7), the latter is not as unacceptable as (5) is. This suggests that the fronting of adverbials is not as dislocating, perceptually, as the fronting of object NP's. That perceptual complexity indeed governs this behavior is further suggested by the fact that as the fronted adverbial grows in length, the obligatory nature of the resumptive pronoun increases. Thus, compare (7) and (8) above with:

(9) **ha-ish SHE-etmol baerev axarey she-Yoav azav ba hena*
      'the-man THAT-yesterday evening after that-Yoav left came here'

(10) *ha-ish SHE-etmol baerev axarey she-Yoav azav HU ba hena*
      'the-man THAT-yesterday evening after THAT-Yoav left HE came here'

      'The man who came here yesterday evening after Yoav left.'

---

[2]This fronting device is used for topicalization. For further details, see Givón (1973).

The data above may be explained readily in terms of perceptual complexity and, in particular, a perceptual preference to the neutral S-V-O word order in Hebrew. When the neutral order is maintained, as in (1) and (3), the resumptive pronoun is redundant, since the head noun is coreferent to the subject of the relative clause and thus the order S-V-O on the surface is maintained. The fronting of constituents which normally come after the verb breaks this perceptual generalization, especially if those constituents are large, as in (9). The use of the resumptive pronoun then makes it possible to recover the subject of the embedded clause, especially with the extensive gender-number agreement in Hebrew.

Finally, as will be shown below the subordinator *she-* may be deleted in object-NP relativization under specified conditions. No deletion of this kind is possible in subject relativization. This is again easy to explain in terms of the data considered above. If the neutral S-V-O order is preserved and thus no resumptive pronoun is used, the omission of the subordinator *she-* will eliminate all clues to the clause being an embedded one, and it can be readily interpreted as a simplex sentence. Thus, compare (11) below to (1) above:

(11)   *ha-ish ba hena etmol baerev*
       'The man came here yesterday evening'

On the other hand, if a resumptive subject pronoun is introduced and then the subordinator *she-* deleted, the construction fully resembles a topicalized structure and is again not interpreted as an embedded clause, i.e.:

(12)   *ha-ish, HU ba hena etmol baerev*
       'the-man, HE came here yesterday evening'

       'As to the man, he came here yesterday evening'

The same thing occurs when a post-verbal constituent is fronted:

(13)   *ha-ish, etmol baerev HU ba hena*
       'the-man, yesterday evening HE came here'

       'As to the man, yesterday evening he came here'

3. ACCUSATIVE-OBJECT-NP RELATIVIZATION

Definite direct objects in Hebrew are marked with the accusative pre-position *et*. In relativization, the use of *et* with the resumptive pronoun does not necessarily involve definite head nouns or their coreferents within the relative clause. Thus fully corresponds to the use of pronouns in English relativization, where the head noun may be indefinite or even non-referential, as in (15) below:

(14)   *eyni mexapes et ha-isha she-tamid roim OTA kan*
       'I-don't seek acc. the-woman that-always (they) see ACC.-HER here'

       'I'm not looking for the woman that one always sees here' (ref.)

(15)   *eyni mexapes (af) isha she-tamid roim OTA kan*
       'I-don't seek (any) woman that-always (they) see ACC.-HER here'

       'I'm not looking for any woman that one always sees here' (non-ref.)

There exists a trade-off between the deletability of the resumptive pronoun in direct-object relativization and the deletability of the subordinator *she-*. When *she-* is present, the resumptive pronoun is optional:

(16) *ha-ish SHE-raiti OTO etmol*   'The man I saw yesterday'
      'the-man THAT-I-say HIM yesterday'

(17) *ha-ish SHE-raiti etmol*   'The man I saw yesterday'
      'the-man THAT-I-saw yesterday'

As long as the resumptive pronoun remains in its neutral post-verbal position, the subordinator *she-* may not be deleted:

(18) **ha-ish raiti OTO etmol*
      'the-man I-saw HIM yesterday'

This is readily explained, since (18) may be easily confused with the topicalized-object construction (19), differing from it only by the presence of a pause:

(19) *ha-ish, raiti OTO etmol*
      'the-man, I-saw HIM yesterday

      'As to the man, I saw him yesterday'

The subordinator is thus indispensible here in signalling the grammatical functions and relations within the utterance. When the resumptive pronoun is fronted, however, the subordinator may be deleted--since its function has now been assumed by the resumptive pronoun:

(20) *ha-ish SHE-OTO raiti etmol*   'The man I saw yesterday'
      'the-man THAT-HIM I-saw yesterday'

(21) *ha-ish OTO raiti etmol*   'The man I saw yesterday'
      'the-man HIM I-saw yesterday'

It is interesting to note that once the neutral S-V-O order is further tampered with, say through the fronting of an adverbial or an indirect object NP, the syntactic freedom of both deletion and pronoun attraction is rapidly lost:

(22) *ha-ish SHE-etmol ba-erev raiti OTO*   (fronted adverb)
      'the-man THAT-yesterday evening I-saw HIM'

      'The man I saw yesterday evening'

(23) *? ha-ish SHE-etmol baerev raiti*   (? pronoun deletion)

(24) **ha-ish SHE-OTO etmol baerev raiti*   (*pronoun attraction)

(25) **ha-ish SHE-etmol baerev OTO raiti*   (*pronoun attraction)

(26) **ha-ish OTO etmol baerev raiti*   (*subordinator deletion)

This again shows how word order and morphological clues (such as pronouns and subordinators) form an interlocking, mutually dependent system vis-a-vis the syntactic/perceptual complexity of the utterance. Increased freedom on one side (here in word order) results in decreased freedom on the other.[3]

─────────────────────

[3]One may perhaps hypothesize that there exists an optimal constant, expressed by the multiple: COMPLEXITY x FREEDOM or perhaps COMPLEXITY x EXPRESSIVE POWER for each construction type in language.

4. RELATIVIZATION OF SIMPLE PREPOSITIONAL NP'S

For reasons that will soon become apparent, the prepositional cases in Hebrew will be divided here into two groups, simple and complex. The simple prepositions, to be discussed in this section, include the bound prepositions ℓ- 'to', m- 'from', b- 'in', 'at', 'by' and the un-bound $e\ell$ 'to', 'toward' and $a\ell$ 'on' (and perhaps also im/it- 'with', whose status is at the moment not fully clear to me). It will be shown below that in some respects the unbound $e\ell$ and $a\ell$ form a sub-group within simple prepositions. For the most part, however, their be-havior corresponds to that of the bound prepositions. For the purpose of the discussion here, only ℓ- 'to will be used, as a representative example.

Unlike accusative et- pronouns, the indirect-object pronouns discussed here may not be option-ally deleted under normal conditions. Though if the pronoun is fronted (attracted), the subordinator she- may still be deleted:

(27)   *ha-ish SHE-natati LO et ha-sefer*
       'the-man THAT-I-gave HIM acc. the-book'

       'The man to whom I gave the book'

(28)   **ha-ish natati LO et ha-sefer*   (*subordinator deletion)

(29)   **ha-ish SHE-natati et ha-sefer*   (*pronoun deletion)

(30)   *ha-ish SHE-LO natati et ha-sefer*
       'the-man THAT-HIM I-gave acc. the-book'

       'The man to whom I gave the book'

(31)   *ha-ish LO natati et ha-sefer*   (subordinator deletion with pronoun
       'the-man HIM I-gave acc. the-book'   fronting)

       'The man to whom I gave the book'

Thus the accusative seems to have more syntactic freedom than the "indirect" prepositional cases, and this must be ultimately explained in terms of psychological or perceptual com-plexity. Notice that the more simplistic perceptual explanation in terms of number of nominals involved on the surface of the utterance will not do here, since if the verb $kr?$ 'call' is used, one which requires only one object nominal in the indirect case ℓ- 'to', the restric-tions still hold:

(32)   *ha-ish she-karati LO*   'The man whom I called'
       'the-man THAT-I-called HIM'

(33)   **ha-ish karati LO*   (*subordinator deletion)

(34)   **ha-ish SHE-karati*   (*pronoun deletion)

(35)   *ha-ish SHE-LO karati*   'The man whom I called'
       'the-man THAT-HIM I-called'

(36)   *ha-ish LO karati*   (subordinator deletion with pronoun
       'the-man HIM I-called'   fronting)

       'The man whom I called'

There are grounds to believe that the non-deletability of the resumptive pronouns here in-volves the bound preposition rather than the resumptive pronoun per-se. There is in fact a special case in which the resumptive pronoun in this type of relativization may be optionally

deleted. This involves a situation in which (a) the head noun modified by the clause is
itself in a prepositional case, and in addition (b) the prepositional case of the head noun is
identical to that of its coreferent noun within the relative clause:

(37)   *1-a-ish SHE-natati LO et ha-sefer eyn avoda*
        'to-the-man to whom I gave HIM acc. the-book no work'[4]

        'The man to whom I gave the book has no work'

(38)   *1-a-ish SHE-natati et ha-sefer eyn avoda*   (pronoun deleted)

        'The man to whom I gave the book has no work'

It is interesting to note that the identity required here is not strict semantic identity, but
rather surface form identity. This is evident from the following example. The preposition
b- in Hebrew is highly polysemous, corresponding to locative cases such as 'in', 'at', 'on',
instrumental-agentive cases such as 'with', 'by' as well as a number of more abstract "dative"
cases. The verb *bxr* 'choose', for example, takes the dative *b-* case. Now consider (39)
below, which is structurally analogous to (38), and where the resumptive pronoun has been
optionally deleted. The coreferent noun within the relative clause is in the dative *b-* case,
while the head noun is in the locative *b-* 'at', 'in' case:

(39)   *b-a-makom SHE-baxarnu eyn avoda*
        'In-the-place THAT-we-chose no work'

        'In the place that we chose there's no work'

These data, I believe, throw interesting light on the nature of the perceptual problem involved in this case. In order to dispense with the resumptive pronoun, the prepositional case
of that pronoun must be recoverable from the surface of the utterance. The surface form of
the preposition which marks the head noun aids in this recovery, since in form it is identical
to the preposition marking the now-deleted coreferent noun. Once the surface form is recovered,
however, the speech perceiver must still recover the semantics of the deleted prepositional
case, which is different in this case. This is most likely recovered from the nature of the
verb involved in the embedded clause.

That the restriction on the deletability of "indirect" resumptive pronouns stems from the need
to recover the prepositional case itself is also evident from the following data. Consider the
unambiguous (40) and (41) below, which share the same verb but have a dative object in two
different cases (*m-* 'from' and *l-* 'for', respectively). If a sentence such as (42) were
allowed in Hebrew, it would be ambiguous with respect to whether it corresponded to (40) or
(41):

(40)   *ha-ish SHE-MIMENO kaniti et ha-sefer*
        'the-man THAT-FROM-HIM I-bought acc. the-book'

        'The man from whom I bought the book'

(41)   *ha-ish SHE-LO kaniti et ha-sefer*
        'the-man THAT-TO-HIM I-bought acc. the-book'

        'The man for whom I bought the book'

(42)   **ha-ish SHE-kaniti et ha-sefer*   (*pronoun deletion)

---

[4]The semantic equivalent of 'NP$_i$ have NP$_{ii}$' is in Hebrew 'to NP$_i$ be NP$_{ii}$'.

Finally, notice that if the prepositional case of the head noun is not surface-identical with that of the coreferent noun within the relative clause, the resumptive pronoun may not be deleted:

(43)   *l-a-ish SHE-MIMENO kaniti et ha-sefer eyn avoda*
        'to-the-man THAT-FROM-HIM I-bought acc. the-book no work'

        'The man from whom I bought the book has no work'

(44)   *l-a-ish SHE-kaniti et ha-sefer eyn avoda[5]*   (*pronoun deletion)

(45)   *me-ha-ish SHE-LO maxarti et ha-sefer kibalti mexir tov*
        'from-the-man THAT-TO-HIM I-sold acc. the-book I-got good price'

        'I got a good price from the man to whom I sold the book'

(46)   *me-ha-ish SHE-maxarti et ha-sefer kibalti mexir tov*   (*pronoun deletion)

I have mentioned above that the bound prepositions *el* and *al* form a distinct sub-group within the simple prepositions. They both allow the deletion of the subordinator *she-* if the resumptive pronoun is attracted:

(47)   *ha-ish ELAV dibarti etmol*   'The man to whom I spoke yesterday'
        'the-man TO-HIM I-spoke yesterday'

(48)   *ha-ish ALAV dibarnu etmol*   'The man about whom we spoke yesterday'
        'the-man ABOUT-HIM we spoke yesterday

However, neither preposition allows the deletion of the resumptive pronoun even when the head noun is in the same prepositional case:[6]

(49)   *el ha-ish SHE-ELAV dibarti etmol bau orxim hayom*
        'to-the-man THAT-TO-HIM I-spoke yesterday came guests today'

        'Guests came today to the man to whom I spoke yesterday'

(50)   *el ha-ish SHE-dibarti etmol bau orxim hayom*

(51)   *al ha-shulxan SHE-ALAV yashavnu yesh sefer*
        'on the-table THAT-ON-IT we-sat there's book'

        'There's a book on the table on which we sat'

(52)   *al ha-shulxan SHE-yashavnu yesh sefer*

It may well be that morphologically unbound prepositions are perceptually more complex in speech processing than their bound counterparts. In purely semantic terms I see no difference between *el*, *al* and the other simple preposition discussed above. It may also be that diachronic considerations may play some role in determining their syntactic freedom. At any rate, if one views obligatoriness as a lessening of syntactic freedom, then one may establish for the simple Hebrew prepositional cases the following hierarchy of syntactic freedom:

---

[5]This sentence is of course perfectly acceptable under another interpretation, ie.e 'The man FOR whom I bought the book...', but not under the interpretation 'from'.

[6]Some speakers find (50) and (52) more acceptable than I do. This may indicate that for them at least the prepositions *el*, *al* have become less complex and now correspond to the bound prepositions.

(53)   *et* (accusative) > *l-*, *b-*, *m-* (bound dative) > *el*, *al*   (free dative)

This hierarchy will be further discussed later on.

5. RELATIVIZATION OF COMPLEX PREPOSITIONAL NP'S

The prepositions discussed in this section bear clear marks of their diachronic origin. Their surface form still displays the structure of genitival noun compounds:

(54)   PREP-NOUN-GEN-

This explains several anachronisms in the grammar of the nouns modified by these complex prepositions. Sometimes these nouns appear with the preposition *l-* 'to', as in:

(55)   *mi-taxat l-a-shulxan*   'under the table'
       'from-bottom-of to-the-table'

The same is also attested in the pronominal variation between the more current (56) and the archaic sounding (57):

(56)   *mi-taxt-av*   'under it'
       'from-bottom-of-it'

(57)   *mi-taxat l-o*   'under it'
       'from-bottom-of to-it'

The presence of the preposition *l-* in the "possessor" noun is fully explained by observing that possessive expressions in Hebrew often involve the combination of the subordinator *she-* (historically *asher*, see discussion later on) and the dative preposition *l-*, as in:

(58)   *ha-shulxan she-l-i*   'my table'
       'the-table that-to-me'

(59)   *ha-shulxan she-l David*   'David's table'[7]
       'the-table that-to David'

The lexical identity of many of the locational nouns involved in forming these complex prepositions is often discernible, and for further discussion of the rather universal processes through which locational nouns participate in the diachronic rise of complex prepositions, see Givón (1971). Prepositions of this type are often "syntactically in transition," and may display mixed and sometime contradictory grammatical behavior. Sometimes they behave semantically like simple prepositions, while syntactically they retain some of the characteristics of the more complex constructions from which they arise. In Hebrew this group involves a large number of locative expressions as well as some more abstract prepositions. A representative list is given in (60) below:

---

[7]The semantic equivalence 'that be to NP' = 'of NP' is quite in line with the observation made in note 4 above.

(60) NON-LOCATIVE   LOCATIVE

      b-shvil-   'for'   *l-fn-*   'in front', 'before'

      b-glal-   'because'   *m-axr-*   'behind'

      l-maan-   'for'   *m-taxt-*   'under' (plus *l-*)

      l-xvod-   'in honor'   *m-al-*   'above'   ,

      b-ad-   'for'   *m-saviv-*   'around' (plus *l-*)

                                        b-emtza-   'in the middle'

                                        b-/m-tsad-   'at the side'

                                        l-yad-   'near'

                                        b-kirva-   'near'

                                        b-mkom-   'instead'

Since a genitival construction is always involved in these prepositions, and since the relativization pattern for nominals in these cases closely follows that of genitival constructions, a short diversion concerning the latter may be in order. Genitivals in Hebrew and their relativization present a close analogue to Ross's (1967) Complex NP environments. Hebrew relativizes on genitives through the use of resumptive pronouns, a pattern which is not available in English:

(61) *ha-ish SHE-et ha-isha SHE-LO raiti etmol*
      'the-man THAT-acc. the-wife THAT-TO-HIM I-saw yesterday'

      'The man whose wife I saw yesterday'

(62) *ha-ish SHE-et ish-T-O raiti etmol*
      'the-man THAT-acc. wife-GEN-HIM I-saw yesterday'

      'The man whose wife I saw yesterday'

(63) *The man that I saw his wife yesterday

The relativization of nominals marked with complex prepositions represents a similar apparent violation of the Complex NP constraint. It is thus not surprising that the syntactic freedom in this type of relativization is extremely limited as compared to other prepositonal cases. As shown in Givón (1973), relativization within complex NP's, though possible in Hebrew, is much more rigidly constrained than simple relativization. One option that is lost here is the deletability of the subordinator *she-* --even when the complex resumptive pronoun is attracted:

(64) *ha-ish SHE-asiti et ze BISHVILO*
      'the-man THAT-I-did acc. this FOR-HIM'

      'The man for whom I did it'

(65) *ha-ish SHE-BISHVILO asiti et ze*
      'the-man THAT-FOR-HIM I-did this'

      'The man for whom I did it'

(66) *ha-ish BISHVILO asiti et ze*   (*subordinator deletion)

This pattern fully parallels that of the genitive:

(67) *ha-ish SHE-raiti et ish-TO*
      'the-man THAT-I-saw acc. wife-GEN-HIM'

      'The man whose wife I saw'

(68)   *ha-ish SHE-et ish-TO raiti*
     'the-man THAT-acc. wife-GEN-HIM I-saw'

     'The man whose wife I saw'

(69)   **ha-ish et ish-TO raiti*   (subordinator deletion)

In addition, the other syntactic option, that of deleting the resumptive pronoun if the head noun is marked by the same preposition, has also been lost in the relativization of complex prepositional nominals. Thus:

(70)   *bishvil ha-ish SHE-BISHVILO asiti et ze lo higia shum davar*
     'for the-man THAT-FOR-HIM I-did acc. this no arrived any thing'

     'Nothing arrived for the man for whom I did it'

(71)   **bishvil ha-ish SHE-asiti et ze lo higia shum davar*

To sum up then, complex prepositions in Hebrew behave just like Complex-NP environments, i.e. as embedded structures. It is only natural then that they exhibit much less syntactic freedom than that shown by simple prepositions.

6. SOME RECENT TRENDS IN RELATIVIZATION

In many languages and many areas of grammar one may observe diachronic changes through which inflected ("agreeing") morphemes eventually give way to invariant (uninflected) ones. In Hebrew this is evident in other areas of the grammar, as in e.g. the replacement of inflected adjectival quantifiers with uninflected pre-nominal ones:

(71a) *anashim rabim*   →   *harbe anashim*   'many men'

      savlanut meata   →   *meat savlanut*   'little patience'

An interesting change has been taking place in the "street language" dialect of Hebrew, by which the anaphoric resumptive pronouns in relativization are systematically replaced by the corresponding interrogative (WH-) pronouns, the latter being positioned in front of the relative subordinator *she-*. In the examples below this pattern will be represented in (b). For only a few prepositional cases, notably the locative but perhaps some others as well, another variant also exists, in which not the WH- pronouns but rather the corresponding demonstrative pronouns 'there', 'then', 'thus' or 'this' are used. In the examples below this will be represented in (c):

(72) a.   *ha-makom SHE-ELAV bati*   (place)
       'the-place THAT-TO-IT I-came'

       'the place to which I came'

   b.   *(ha-makom) EYFO SHE-bati*
       '(the-place) WHERE THAT-I-came'

       '(the place) where I came'

   c.   *ha-makom SHE-le-sham bati*
       'the-place THAT-to there I-came'

       'the place to where I came'

(73) a.   *ha-yom SHE-BO azavti*   (time)
       'the-day THAT-IN-IT I-left'

       'the day on which I left'

b. (ha-yom) MATAY SHE-azavti
'(the-day) WHEN THAT-I-left'

'(the day) when I left'

c. ? ha-yom SHE-az azavti
'the-day THAT-then I-left'

'the day when I left'

(74) a. ha-tsura SHE-BA asiti et ze   (manner)
'the-way THAT-IN-IT I-did acc. this'

'the way in which I did it'

b. (*ha-tzura) EYX SHE-asiti et ze
'(*the-way) HOW THAT-I-did acc. this'

'how I did it'

c. ? ha-tsura SHE-kaxa asiti et ze
'the-way THAT-thus I-did acc. this'

'the way I did it'

(75) a. ha-siba SHE-BIGLALA bati   (reason)
'the-reason THAT-BECAUSE-OF-IT I-came'

'the reason for which I came'

b. (*ha-siba) LAMA SHE-bati
'(*the-reason) WHY THAT-I-came'

'(the reason) why I came'

(76) a. ha-davar SHE-OTO raiti   (accusative)
'the-thing THAT-IT I-saw'

'the thing that I saw'

b. (ha-davar) MA SHE-raiti
'(the-thing) WHAT THAT-I-saw'

'what I saw'

c. ? ha-davar SHE-et-ze raiti
'the-thing THAT-acc-this I-saw'

'the thing which I saw'

(77) a. ha-ish SHE-OTO raiti   (accusative, human)
'the-man THAT-HIM I-saw'

'the man that I saw'

b. (ha-ish) MI SHE-raiti
'(the-man) WHO THAT-I-saw'

'the one whom I saw'

(78) a. ha-ish SHE-ba hena   (subject case)
'the-man THAT-came here'

'the man who came here'

b. (ha-ish) MI SHE-ba hena
'(the-man) WHO THAT-came here'

'the one who came here'

There are several additional facts to take into consideration. To begin with, there exist--
in some of these cases--blend forms of patterns (a) and (b) above. Thus compare (79) below
with (72):

(79) *ha-makom EYFO SHE-ELAV bati*
      'the-place WHERE THAT-TO-IT I-came'

      'the place to which I came'

In (79) both interrogative and anaphoric-resumptive pronouns are used. An even more common
pattern is a blend of (b) and (c). Thus compare (80) below with (72):

(80) *(ha-makom) EYFO SHE-bati le-sham*
      '(the-place) WHERE THAT-I-came to-there'

      'the place where I went'

In (80) both interrogative and demonstrative-resumptive pronouns are used.

It seems to me that (aside from the blends which are an embarrassment of riches in terms of
available clues and thus are not likely to survive for very long) pattern (c) above is simply
a replacement of the anaphoric with the corresponding demonstrative pronoun--in the function
of resumptive pronoun. The pattern is thus of more limited interest.

The (b) pattern, involving the WH- pronouns, is of much more interest. To begin with, it is
more widespread in Hebrew. It is also attested in English as well as in a number of other
Indo-European languages. There are several interesting aspects worth elaboration here. First,
note that in this pattern the presence of a head noun in many cases has become either optional
or simply proscribed. This pattern in English is much more limited, being confined only to
'what', as in:

(81) *what I saw*

Next, the more common pattern in Hebrew when the head noun is used, is to condense the interrogative pronoun and the following subordinator *she-* into a single invariant morpheme *mshe-*,
in which the inflectional distinction between *ma* (non-human) and *mi* (human) is totally zeroed
out:

(82) *ha-ish mshe-raiti etmol*   'the man I saw yesterday'

(83) *ha-sefer mshe-raiti etmol*   'the book I saw yesterday'

Not unexpectedly, this pattern allows the inflected anaphoric-resumptive pronoun to appear--
but only in the post-verb position, never in the attracted position:

(84) *ha-ish mshe-raiti OTO*   'the man I saw'
      'the-man WH-THAT-I-saw HIM'

(85) **ha-ish mshe-OTO raiti*

The inacceptability of (85) may be simply explained by a top-heavy situation at the point
separating the head noun from the embedded clause, where now not one but three adjacent signals
are available to separate the one from the other. Notice, further, that in full accord with
what was observed in the preceding sections, the resumptive pronoun in the case of indirect
object relativization under this pattern is obligatory:

(86) *ha-ish m-she-natati LO et ha-sefer*   'the man to whom I gave the book'
      'the-man WH-THAT-I gave HIM acc. the-book'

(87) **ha-ish m-she-natati et ha-sefer*   (*pronoun deletion)

Of considerable interest is the diachronic process through which WH-pronouns invade the signalling system of relativization and eventually fuse with the erstwhile relative subordinator.
This is occurring now in Hebrew and has presumably occurred in English and Romance. Since
this diachronic trend has a certain measure of universality, natural explanations for it should
be sought. One which I would like to REJECT at the very start is the one which suggests THAT
THE ORIGIN OF THE SEEMING ETYMOLOGICAL RELATION BETWEEN RELATIVE AND INTERROGATIVE PRONOUNS
LIES IN THE FACT THAT RELATIVIZATION (OR PRESUPPOSITION, IN SEMANTIC TERMS) IS ALWAYS INVOLVED
IN THE UNDERLYING STRUCTURE OF WH-QUESTIONS. So that interrogative pronouns resemble relative
pronouns because they were "borrowed" from relativization. As attractive as this analysis may
sound at first, I think it is not supported by facts. To begin with, the etymology in both
Hebrew and English support the opposite direction of borrowing. Further, in all languages in
which this development has taken place, I believe one could show that at an earlier stage no
relative pronouns existed at all. Rather, there existed a relative subordinator and anaphoric-
resumptive pronouns in relativization, and a separate set of WH-pronouns for questions.

The other alternative, to my mind more fruitful, is to try and explain the diachronic change in
the opposite direction. Thus, for example, the WH- pattern of relative subordination has
existed in a number of other constructions in Hebrew for much longer. One of those is the
environment of embedded questions, as in complements of verbs of cognition ('know') or utterance ('say', 'ask'). This pattern is particularly obvious in non-factive contexts, i.e. those
of uncertainty or negativity. (It is not unreasonable to assume that querries form a natural
sub-set of these environments. For some discussion of this, see Givón (1973)). Thus, consider the following expressions from Hebrew:

(88)   *ani yodea eyfo (she-) hu nimtsa*   'I know where he is'
       'I know where (that-) he is'

(89)   *ani lo yodea matay (she-) hu yavo*   'I don't know when he'll come'
       'I no know when (that-) he will-come'

(90)   *'ani hisbarti lo eyx (she-) hi tagia*   'I explained to him how she'll come'
       'I explained to-him how (that-) she will-come'

(91)   *shaalti oto ma (she-) hi amra*   'I asked him what she said'
       'I-asked him what (that-) she said'

In the pattern of (88)-(91) above the subordinator *she-* was optional and in fact redundant.
Notice, however, that these embedded questions may be paraphrased by their corresponding--and
expanded--pseudo-cleft counterparts. In that pattern, the underlying relativization involved
in WH-questions is made more obvious--and the (relative) subordinator *she-* becomes obligatory.
Thus, (92) below paraphrases (91):

(92)   *shaalti oto ma ze haya she-hi amra*   'I asked him what it was that she said'
       'I-asked him what this was that-she said'

(93)   **shaalti oto ma ze haya hi amra*

A fully parallel case may be seen in unembedded WH- questions. Thus below, (94), (95) and
(96) are paraphrases, while (97)--in which *she-* has been deleted, is ungrammatical:

(94)   *ma hi amra?*   'What did she say?'
       'what she said'

(95)   *ma ze she-hi amra?*   'What was it that she said?'
       what this that-she said'

(96)   *ma ze haya she-hi amra?*   'What was it that she said?'
       'what this was that-she said'

(97)   *ma ze haya hi amra*

If one may venture a guess, the optional presence of the relative subordinator *she-* in embedded WH- questions in Hebrew is simply a leftover from an earlier stage when the WH-
question appeared in its more expanded form, including a relative clause.

Another environment where the combination of WH-pronouns and the relative subordinator appears
is in indefinite and non-referential expressions such as:

  (98)   *matay she-lo yihye*   'whenever it be'
         'when that-no be'

  (99)   *mi she-yavo yavo*   'whoever comes comes'
         'who that-come come'

  (100) *taase et ze eyx she-hu*   'do it somehow'
         'you-do acc. this how that-be'

  (101) *lo mexake lexa mi-she-hu?*   'Isn't someone waiting for you?'
         'no waiting you who-that-be

  (102) *nimtsa et ze eyfo she-hu*   'We'll find it somewhere'
         'we-find acc. this where that-be

I think the data above, though not complete, suggest the following hypothesis:

  (a) The subordinator *she-* appears in WH- questions, embedded or otherwise, because
       relativization was involved in those constructions;

  (b) WH-pronouns appear in indefinites such as in (98)-(102) because of some underlying
       semantic unity of uncertainty (or "non-factive") contexts. It is perhaps possible
       that these pronouns should be characterized as NON-REFERENTIAL rather than "inter-
       rogative";

  (c) Finally, the use of interrogative pronouns in relativization spread later on from
       either embedded WH-questions or other non-referential expressions containing both
       WH- pronouns and the relative subordinator.

Another fact seems to lend credence to part (c) of the hypothesis. In many languages the same
morpheme serves as subordinator for both relative clauses and verb complements--particularly
those of cognition and utterance verbs ('know', 'say'). In Hebrew this particle is *she-*,
whose etymology goes back to *asher* and ultimately to the noun *athar* 'place'. In Aramaic it is
the morpheme *de-*, cognate to the Hebrew demonstrative *ze* 'this'. In English it is the demonstrative 'that'. In Spanish it is the interrogative pronoun *que*. It may well be that this
parallelism establishes a precedent, along whose lines it is easy to analogize from verb
complements to relative clauses. Whether this parallelism has further significance, either
synchronically or diachronically, remains to be seen.

7. CONCLUSION

The data brought out in this paper lend, I believe, further support to hypotheses developed
previously concerning the syntactic-perceptual role of the various morphological clues used
in relativization. It further supports claims made by Keenan (1972) and Givón (1973) concerning the role resumptive pronouns play in simplifying the perceptual complexity of
relative clauses. It furnishes further evidence to the claims developed in Givón (1973)
concerning the inverse relation between syntactic complexity and syntactic freedom in language.
These observations also fit well with those made by Emonds (1971) about the prevalence of much
stricter syntactic constraints on movement transformations (or, in my terms, on word-order
freedom) in embedded clauses as compared with main clauses. Many of the root-transformations

dealt with by Emonds (1971) involve "stylistic" devices related to the area of topic-comment
assignment. One may thus argue, as I have done in Givón (1973), that language allows more
EXPRESSIVE POWER in main clauses since they are perceptually easier to process--and also (with
some exceptions; for this see Hooper and Thompson, 1973) because the bulk of the new information presented in the utterance is found in the main clause. The more deeply embedded
clauses, such as relative clauses and verb complements, on the other hand, tend to contain the
older, presupposed, background information. It seems to me, then, that the key to understand-
ing the phenomena discussed here involves the governing role of perceptual complexity.
Language seems to tend towards concentrating the new information in less-complex constructions
with more syntactic options that are responsible for more expressive power.

Of great interest are the differences in syntactic freedom found here between the various
cases of nominals associated with the verb. It seems to me that several hierarchies should
be discussed here separately. The first involves, for S-V-O languages at least, the hierarchy
of:

  (103)   NOMINATIVE (agent) > ACCUSATIVE (patient) > DATIVE (goal)

It was shown above that there is a definite decrease in syntactic freedom along this line.
This must correspond to two other hierarchized dimentions: PSYCHOLOGICAL COMPLEXITY and
SEMANTIC PROMINENCE. In this connection notice that, again at least for S-V-O languages,
the hierarchy of syntactic freedom (103) is exactly the converse of the hierarchy of morphological markedness. One may perhaps argue that the subject-agent case (a) has the highest
semantic import, and therefore (b) is put in the perceptually least complex position and
thus (c) needs less overt morphological marking to distinguish it.

The other hierarchy that is of interest is the one observed for the various "indirect" prepositional cases in Hebrew:

  (104)   *bound-simple > unbound-simple > complex*

For the complex prepositions, it is quite clear that to a great extent they are still analysed,
perceptually, as complex, embedded structures. There are grounds to believe, however, that
the simple prepositions of Hebrew also arose, diachronically, from a genitival noun-compound
origin. For more universal grounds in support of such a hypothesis, see Givón (1971). More
specific in this case is the fact that the pronouns attached to the simple prepositions are
etymologically, without exception, the GENITIVAL pronouns. And this is true for all Semitic
languages. One may thus argue that the bound simple prepositions represent the OLDER LAYER
diachronically, and have been reduced, quite expectedly, to only single consonants bound to
stems. The unbound *el* and *al* represent a slightly later action, and have not yet been fully
reduced. What is intriguing about the data discussed here, is the suggestion that perhaps
the re-analysing of the perceptual-psychological complexity of the various "generations" of
prepositions occurs gradually over time, and that the more recently introduced "generation"
is still perceived as being--in whatever terms this is meaningful--more complex.

REFERENCES

Emonds, J. (1971), *Structure preserving and root transformation*, PhD dissertation, MIT (available from Indian Linguistic Club).

Givón, T. (1971), "Historical syntax and synchronic morphology: An archaeologist's field trip," *CLS #7*, University of Chicago.

Givón, T. (1972), "A note on subject postposing," *Studies in African Linguistics*, 3.2.

Givón, T. (1973), "Complex NP's, word order and resumptive pronouns in Hebrew," *CLS #9*, Parasession volume, University of Chicago.

Givón, T. (1973), "Opacity and reference in language: An inquiry into the role of modalities," in J. Kimball (ed.), *Syntax and Semantics*, vol. II, Seminar Press, NY.

Hooper, J. and S. Thompson (1973), "On the applicability of root transformations," *Linguistic Inquiry*.

Keenan, E. (1972), "Logic, and the expressive power of natural language," *Daedalus*, U.S. Academy of Arts and Sciences.

Ross, J. (1967), *Constraints on variables in Syntax*, PhD dissertation, MIT.

FIRST NORTH-AMERICAN CONFERENCE ON SEMITIC LINGUISTICS

Santa Barbara, California
March 24-25, 1973

The first North-American Conference on Semitic Linguistics was organized by Robert Hetzron (University of California, Santa Barbara) with the cooperation of Giorgio Buccellati (University of California, Los Angeles) and Joseph L. Malone (Barnard College--Columbia University). The purpose of the Conference is to promote the interest of Semitists in the various modern currents of linguistics. The full list of the papers presented at the 1973 Conference is given below. Those papers which have been submitted and accepted for inclusion in *AAL*, like the present one, are being published within the framework of the journal.

A. Semitic and its Afroasiatic Cousins

1. Carleton T. Hodge (University of Indiana), *The Nominal Sentence in Semitic* (=*AAL* 2/4).
2. G. Janssens (University of Ghent, Belgium), *The Semitic Verbal System* (=*AAL* 2/4).
3. J. B. Callender (UCLA), *Afroasiatic Cases and the Formation of Ancient Egyptian Verbal Constructions with Possessive Suffixes* (=*AAL* 2/6).
4. Russell G. Schuh (UCLA), *The Chadic Verbal System and its Afroasiatic Nature* (forthcoming in *AAL*).
5. Andrzej Zaborski (University of Cracow, Poland), *The Semitic External Plural in an Afroasiatic Perspective* (forthcoming in *AAL*).

B. Ancient Semitic Languages

6. Giorgio Buccellati (UCLA), *On the Akkadian "Attributive" Genitive* (forthcoming in *AAL*).
7. Daniel Ronnie Cohen (Columbia University), *Subject and Object in Biblical Aramaic: A Functional Approach Based on Form-Content Analysis* (=*AAL* 2/1).
8. Richard Steiner (Touro College, N.Y.), *Evidence from a Conditioned Sound Change for Lateral ḍ in Pre-Aramaic.*
9. Stanislav Segert (UCLA), *Verbal Categories of Some Northwest Semitic Languages: A Didactical Approach* (=*AAL* 2/5).
10. Charles Krahmalkov (University of Michigan), *On the Noun with Heavy Suffixes in Punic.*

C. Hebrew

11. Joseph L. Malone (Barnard College--Columbia University), *Systematic vs. Autonomous Phonemics and the Hebrew Grapheme "dagesh"* (=*AAL* 2/7).
12. Allan D. Corré (University of Wisconsin, Milwaukee), *"Wāw" and "Digamma"* (forthcoming in *AAL*).
13. Harvey Minkoff (Hunter College, N.Y.), *A Feature Analysis of the Development of Hebrew Cursive Scripts* (=*AAL* 1/7).
14. Raphael Nir (Hebrew University, Jerusalem), *The Survival of Obsolete Hebrew Words in Idiomatic Expressions* (=*AAL* 2/3).
15. Talmy Givón (UCLA), *On the Role of Perceptual Clues in Hebrew Relativization* (=*AAL* 2/8).
16. Alan C. Harris (UCLA), *The Relativization "which that is" in Israeli Hebrew.*

D. Arabic

17. Ariel A. Bloch (University of California, Berkeley), *Direct and Indirect Relative Clauses in Arabic.*
18. Frederic J. Cadora (Ohio State University), *Some Features of the Development of Telescoped Words in Arabic Dialects and the Status of Koiné II.*

E. Ethiopian

19. Gene B. Gragg (University of Chicago), *Morpheme Structure Conditions and Underlying Form in Amharic* (forthcoming in *AAL*).
20. C. Douglas Johnson (University of California, Santa Barbara), *Phonological Channels in Chaha* (=*AAL* 2/2).
21. Robert Hetzron (University of California, Santa Barbara), *The t-Converb in Western Gurage and the Role of Analogy in Historical Morphology* (=*AAL* 2/2).

F. Beyond Afroasiatic

22. Gilbert B. Davidowitz (New York), *Cognate Afroasiatic and Indoeuropean Affixes: Conjugational Person-Markers.*